MW01503094

Author Fredd Carroll

Also has a Middle School Series

THE ADVENTURES OF
LEFT EYE LAZY

Books 1-4 are available
only on Amazon

https://amzn.to/2EqbVVZ

VSZ PUBLISHING©2020

FREDD CARROLL©2020

This book is dedicated to all the children who love animals.

Especially, Two of my favorite little girls.

Celestine Nelson & Kylie Smithgall

When you see an Animal - it's often known by you.

A cat, a dog, a baby goat - or hopping kangaroo.

But do you know the word to use when hanging with their friends?

In groups of four or five or six or even groups of ten.

A few of them are fun to say and all of them are true.

Like when a <u>MONKEY</u> hangs with friends, this bunch is called A

TROOP

Here is one I never knew and makes my eyebrows raise.

When _RACCOONS_ choose to eat together, this is called a **_GAZE_**

I have a few I really like that I would like to note.

Like when a bunch of HIPPOS huddle this is called a *BLOAT*

Then there is the PORCUPINE and you will laugh like you are tickled.

But when they want to see their pals this group is called a

PRICKLE

When I see their big sharp teeth, I always shake and quiver.

But when SHARKS choose to swim with friends, this swim is called a *SHIVER*

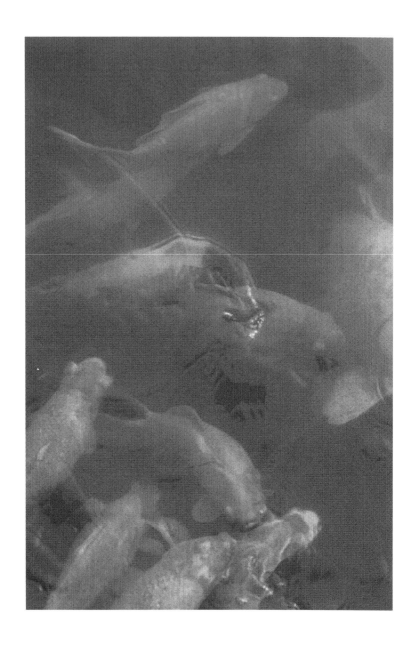

The oceans filled with many things and some ~~FISH~~ look so cool.

Just like you and all your friends this friendship is a

SCHOOL

It's fun to read this story and it's fun to say these words.

Quite a few of many friends are also called a

HERD

<u>ZEBRA</u>, <u>ELK</u> and <u>ELEPHANT</u> who run with buddies free?

I wonder if you know these three.

how many have you seen?

Ten <u>TIGERS</u> are an

AMBUSH

While ten <u>LIONS</u> are a

PRIDE

Both are big and beautiful

But neither safe to ride.

PENGUINS waddle on the ice and look so cute to me.

When they waddle with their pals It's called a

COLONY

<u>PEACOCK</u> feathers look so bright when walking in a cluster. Maybe it is why they say a group of them is **_MUSTER_**

<u>SQUIRRELS</u> will jump and gather nuts, then run mad in a fury.

When they run with other pals it's also called a

SCURRY

<u>MICE</u> in groups a

MISCHIEF when they

gather eating cheese.

The <u>OWLS</u> form a

PARLIAMENT when

sitting in their trees.

When hunting in the snowy woods <u>WOLVES</u> travel in a **PACK**

When <u>JELLYFISH</u> surf on the waves, they call themselves a **SMACK**

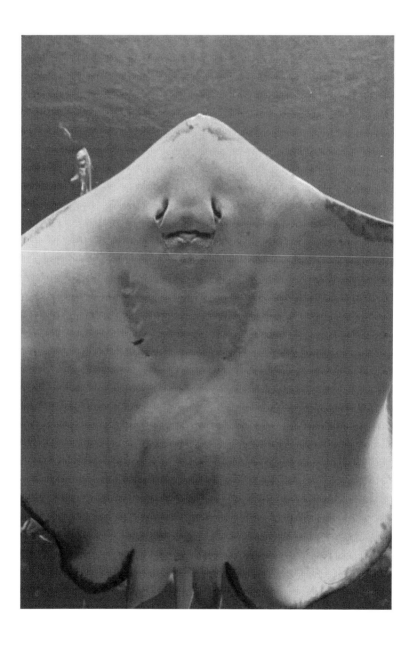

WOMBATS form a

WISDOM

WEASELS prefer

GANG

STINGRAYS are a

FEVER

The HEDGEHOGS an

ARRAY

FROGS hop as an **_ARMY_**

BADGERS are a **_SET_**

I'd love to tell you all of
them

But some I still forget.

A **FLOCK** of BIRDS all fly as friends.

HUMMINGBIRDS a **CHARM**

CHEETAHS in a **COALITION**

BEES fly in a **SWARM**

LIZARDS are a
LOUNGE

DOLPHINS form a
POD

BEAVERS go as
FAMILY

And OTTERS are a
ROMP

A **LEAP** of <u>LEOPARDS</u>
walks together.

<u>CRABS</u> will form a
CAST

<u>ANTS</u> become a
COLONY

And <u>CROCS</u> prefer to
BASK

Before I go, I want to say - it's hard to pick just one.

I hope you learned a thing or two and hope that you had fun.

There's many still and more to see so try to find your own.

Maybe tell me other names that I may not have shown.

Animals are beautiful I love them all the same.

But when they gather in a group, I love their silly names.

Be kind, be sweet and be your best – and smile when you can.

When <u>CAMELS</u> gather in the sand it's called a *CARAVAN*

THE END

Thank you, my little friends. I hope you have a fun, safe day.

Be polite, be nice, be happy.

Fredd Carroll

Made in the USA
Columbia, SC
11 October 2020